Nina,
always follow
your dreams!

Erica Bradshaw

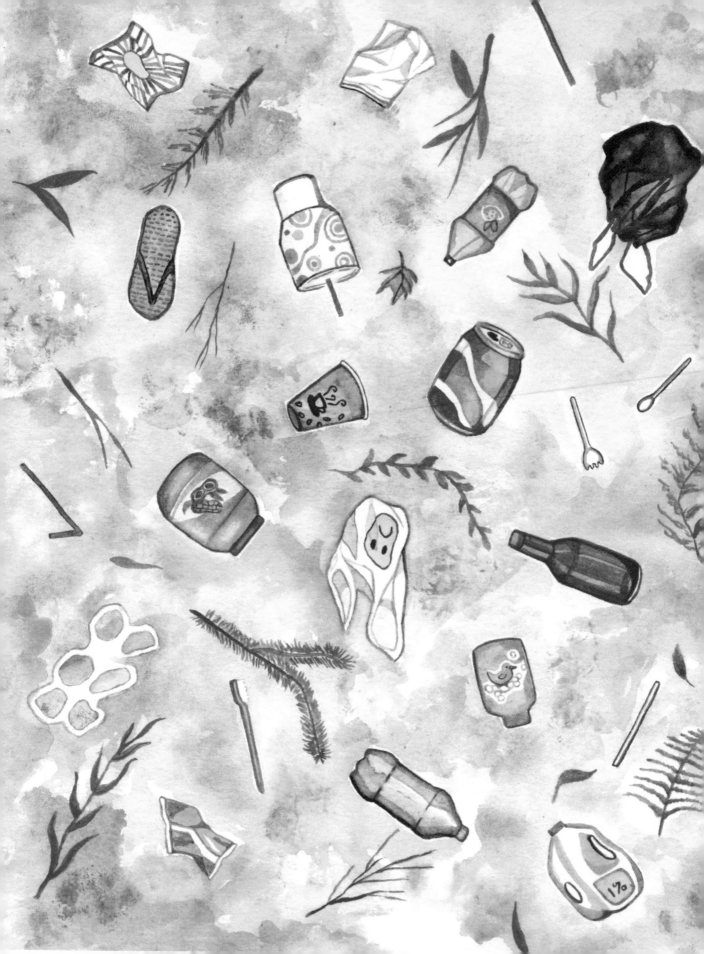

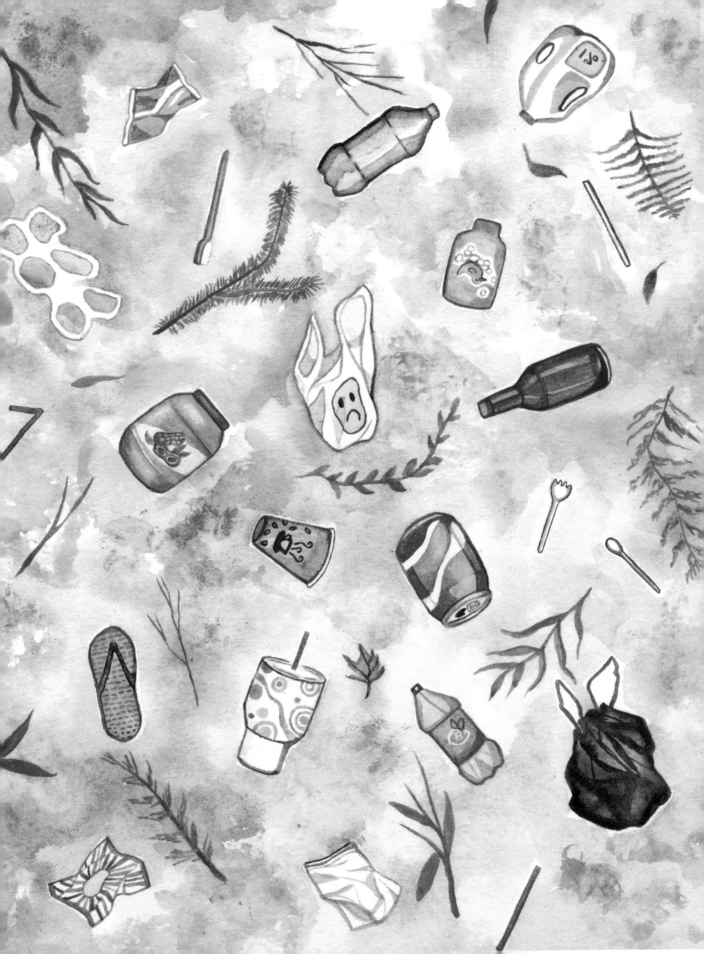

THEIR
HOME,
OUR
LANDFILL

Written and Illustrated by: Erica Bradshaw

Bradshaw, Erica
Their home, Our landfill.
Kalamazoo, Mich.: To Draw Attention Publishing, 2018.
24 pages illustrations
1. Pollution 2. Environment 3. Wildlife
JE BRAD
ISBN: 978-1-7327659-0-0
Book design and layout: Erica Bradshaw & Words by Design, Kalamazoo, Mich.
Printed by LSI

"Environmental pollution is an incurable disease. It can only be prevented." -Barry Commoner

Dedicated to PCCI, Beth Purdy, and all the people who support me in the process of making my dreams a reality.

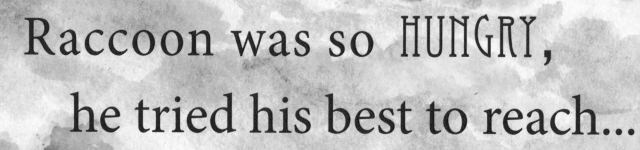

Raccoon was so HUNGRY,
he tried his best to reach...

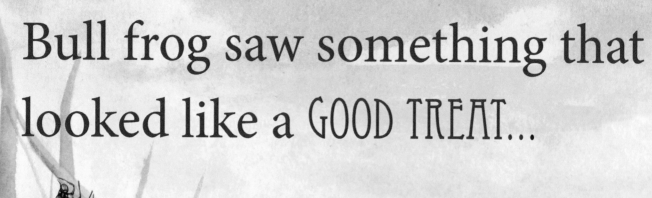

Bull frog saw something that looked like a GOOD TREAT...

Duckling was PLAYING,
but got all wrapped up...

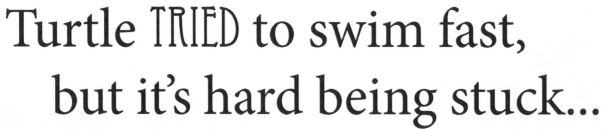

Turtle TRIED to swim fast,
but it's hard being stuck...

Mouse couldn't help it,
he SMELLED something sweet,

Mama brings WARMTH
for babies to sleep...

HOW YOU AND YOUR FAMILY CAN HELP...

USE REUSABLE ITEMS

Since most small plastics, like straws, bottle caps, and plastic bags cannot be recycled, make easy swaps to reusable options!
- Stainless steel straws
- Glass or stainless steel water bottles
- Canvas or cotton bags

GO PLASTIC FREE WHENEVER YOU CAN

Plastic packaging often gets thrown right in the garbage. At the grocery store, bring a light weight fabric or crocheted bag to

weigh fresh produce in to reduce plastic waste.

STAY AWAY FROM STYROFOAM

Recycling facilities rarely accept styrofoam products. When eating out, bring your own container or simply ask for some aluminum foil to wrap your meal in!

BATHROOM TIPS

Switch to these plastic free alternatives in the bathroom:
· All natural toothbrushes made of bamboo can be composted.
· Steel safety razors with single, replaceable blades last a lifetime!
· Shampoo, conditioner, and body washes are offered in bar form. They tend to last longer than the liquid versions and do not require the plastic packaging. Often available in all natural recipes, they are great for healthy hair and skin.

KITCHEN TIPS

· Try reusable containers instead of single use plastic zip seal bags.
· Use naturally antibacterial, beeswax-coated cotton food wrap, rather than plastic cling wrap.
· Make your own cleaning products from natural ingredients such as baking soda, vinegar, castile soap, hydrogen peroxide, and essential oils. Store them in glass spray bottles.

1.REDUCE- what you take in & the amount you use

2.REUSE - what you can

3.REPURPOSE- the "old", into "new"

4.RECYCLE - if unable to do the above

5.RETHINK!- everyday is "Earth Day!" Prevention is key.

ALL ABOUT OUR ANIMAL FRIENDS...

DAMSEL FLIES Did you happen to find these guys along the water's edge throughout the book? They are often found near shallow freshwater. They are not dragonflies, as they are thinner, smaller, and their wings rest together, rather than apart.

RACCOONS are omnivores, meaning they will eat both plants and animals. They find most of their meals by the water and eat bugs, frogs, eggs, and crayfish. When not around water they forage for berries, mice, and find food in our trash! They live in forests, marshes, prairies, and even cities!

BULLFROGS are carnivores meaning they eat other animals. Their meals consist of insects, spiders, mice, small birds, fish, snakes, scorpions, and even other frogs! Considering they eat anything they can find, it wouldn't be surprising if you found a bullfrog eating trash that floated by.

MALLARD DUCKS prefer eating mostly plants. To get their food, they flip upside down on the surface of the water. Male mallard ducks are called drakes and they have a bright green shiny head, where the females are mostly brown. Mama duck can lay up to 12 eggs and nests near the water. A group of her ducklings is called a brood. Almost a day after hatching ducklings run, swim, and search for food on their own. Since ducklings live near the water's edge they can easily be impacted by litter and debris.

all information sourced from: www.livescience.com, www.nationalgeographic.com ,www.audubon.org, www.britannica.com

EASTERN PAINTED TURTLES are omnivores and

will eat plants and insects. Turtles can not remove their shells. Since their shell grows with them their whole life, if they were to get stuck in something they can't get out of, their shell will grow around it. Their hard protective shells wrap around them like armor against animals that try to eat them. Painted turtles love to swim in ponds, rivers, lakes and marshes. You will often see them sunbathing on rocks and fallen tree branches.

FIELD MICE are omnivores and eat about 20 times a day. They will eat about anything they can get their hands on. Unfortunately, this means that they can get trapped in tiny openings trying hard to find their food. Mice are known to burrow in forests, grasslands, and man-made structures. They are nocturnal, meaning they sleep during the day so often you will hear them scuttering around at night time.

CERULEAN WARBLERS are considered threatened,

or endangered, mostly due to a species called the cowbird. This bird invades their nest and lays eggs that spread diseases to the warblers' eggs. Both the male and female warblers unknowingly raise the cowbird eggs and neglect their own. Cerulean warblers nest in forests, and especially in river valleys. One type of tree they like to nest in is the sycamore. Since they nest high up in trees during the summer, they are a less common bird to see. Although these birds nests are hard to observe, many bird's nest with unnatural materials as our urban areas close in on the birds natural environment.

CPSIA information can be obtained
at www.ICGtesting.com
Printed in the USA
LVIC051810070419
613280LV00001B/3

* 9 7 8 1 7 3 2 7 6 5 9 0 0 *